MONSTER JOKE BOOK

compiled by
GORDON HILL

foulsham
LONDON · NEW YORK · TORONTO · SYDNEY

foulsham

Yeovil Road, Slough, Berkshire SL1 4JH

ISBN 0-572-01561-5

Copyright © 1991 W. Foulsham and Co. Ltd

Printed in Great Britain at St. Edmundsbury Press, Bury St. Edmunds, Suffolk.
Phototypeset by Typesetting Solutions, Slough, Berks.

Why did the ghost visit the safari park?

He wanted to be a big game haunter.

How do you get a monster into a matchbox?

Take the matches out.

Why did the monster measure himself?

He wanted to know if he gruesome.

What's big, green and unhappy?

The Incredible Sulk.

What did the monsters do at the wedding?

They toasted the bride and groom.

How does a monster go on a diet?

He only eats pygmies.

What's written on the tombstone of Frankenstein's monster?

Rust in Peace.

Why did the wart-covered, three-eyed monster give up boxing?

He didn't want his looks spoiled.

Why did the monster start buying "Which Magazine"?

He wanted to join the Consumer's Association.

What's the difference between
a monster and a banana?

Ever tried peeling a monster.

Why do some monsters
forget everything you say?

*Because it goes in one ear
and out the others.*

monster with three arms and
five legs went into a clothes
shop and told the manager
"I'd like to see a suit that
would fit me." The manager
took one look and said "So
would I."

Mummy, Mummy, why is Daddy so quiet?

Shut up and keep digging.

What did the river say when the monster sat in it?

Well, I'm damned.

What happened to Frankenstein's monster when it was caught for speeding?

It was fined £30 and dismantled for six months.

Where are monsters found?

Don't know; it's not often they get lost.

How do you flatten a ghost?

Hit it with a spirit level.

What did the policeman say to the three-headed monster?

'Ello, 'ello, 'ello.

What do Red Indians call a
haunted wigwam?

A creepy teepee.

What's a ghost's favourite
drink?

Bier.

Why do monsters buy
newspapers?

To read their horror-scopes.

10

Who was a ghostly French emperor?

Napoleon Boney-parte.

Where do ghosts like to swim?

In the Dead Sea.

What's the best thing to do with a blue monster?

Try to cheer it up.

What do sea monsters eat?

Fish and ships.

Daddy, Daddy — Mummy's fighting with a 20-metre monster!

Don't worry, son — it hasn't got a chance.

How can you tell when there's a monster in your fridge?

The door won't shut.

What's a British ghost's favourite airline?

British Scareways.

First Monster: Why are you standing on one leg?

Second Monster: *Because you just trod on my foot.*

13

Why shouldn't you pull a
monster's tail?

*Because pulling a monster's tail
could be your end.*

*What's the difference between
a monster and a biscuit?*

*Ever tried dunking a monster in
your tea.*

Taxi for the Abominable
Snowman — are you ready,
sir?

Not yeti.

Mummy, Mummy, why is Daddy running so fast?

Shut up and keep shooting.

What's as big as a 200-kilo monster but doesn't weigh anything?

Its shadow.

What do monsters like to eat with bread and cheese?

Pickled organs.

What did the monster do
when he lost his tail?

*He bought a new one from a
re-tailer.*

Why did the six-headed
monster ask for a pay rise?

*Because it had so many
mouths to feed.*

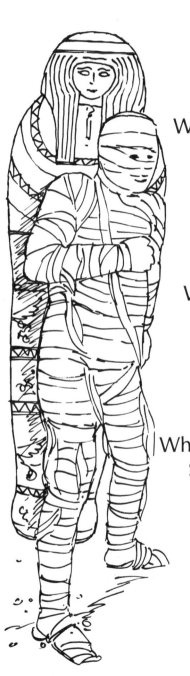

Which French President
was a ghost?

Charles de Ghoul.

What do Abominable
Snowparents have?

Chill-dren.

Where do American ghosts
go for their holidays?

Boo York.

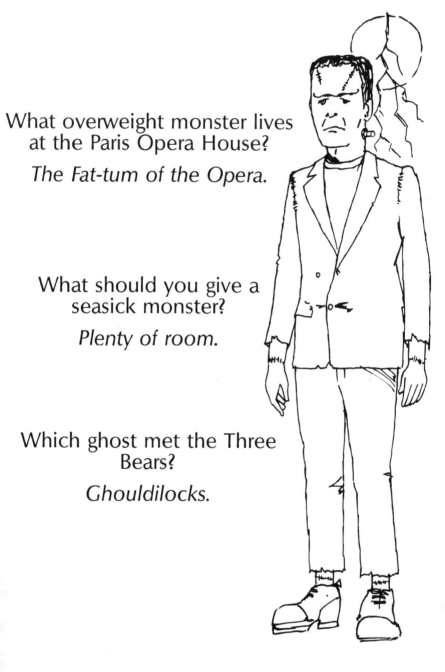

What overweight monster lives at the Paris Opera House?

The Fat-tum of the Opera.

What should you give a seasick monster?

Plenty of room.

Which ghost met the Three Bears?

Ghouldilocks.

Who delivers presents to monsters at Christmas?

Santa Claws.

First Monster: For lunch I'm going to eat everyone in Peking. Like to join me?

Second Monster: *No thanks, I can't stand Chinese food.*

What do you call a monster with three nostrils, one eye, two horns and fangs?

Ugly.

What walks through walls going "er... er... boo"?

A nervous ghost.

What do you call ghosts in an aeroplane?

High spirits.

20

What has fangs, three heads, and flies?

A very dead monster.

Who won the monsters' beauty contest?

No one.

Why was King Kong taken to hospital?

He had ape-endicitis.

What's an American ghost's favourite dessert?

Boo-berry pie.

What do land monsters eat?

Fish and chips.

What's a monster's favourite breakfast?

Scrambled legs and bacon.

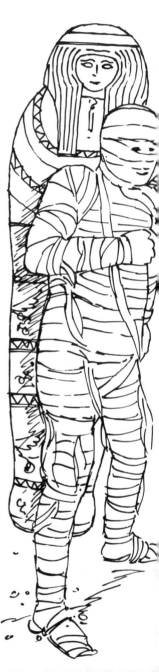

What do you get if you cross a mouse with a monster?

Great big holes in the skirting-board.

What's a ghost's favourite country?

Wails.

What does King Kong's wife
wear in the kitchen?

An ape-ron.

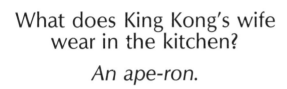

How do ghosts repair their
clothes?

With invisible mending.

What's ugly, weighs 300 kilos
and goes up and down?

A monster in a lift.

What did one ghost say to
the other?

Do you believe in people.

How do you stop monsters
getting under your bed?

Saw the legs off.

How can you tell when there's
a monster under your bed?

*Your nose is pressed against
the ceiling.*

Which monster has the best hearing?

The eeriest.

What's a ghost footballer's favourite position?

Ghoul-keeper.

Boy Monster: What lovely eyes you have.

Girl Monster: *Yes, they were a birthday present.*

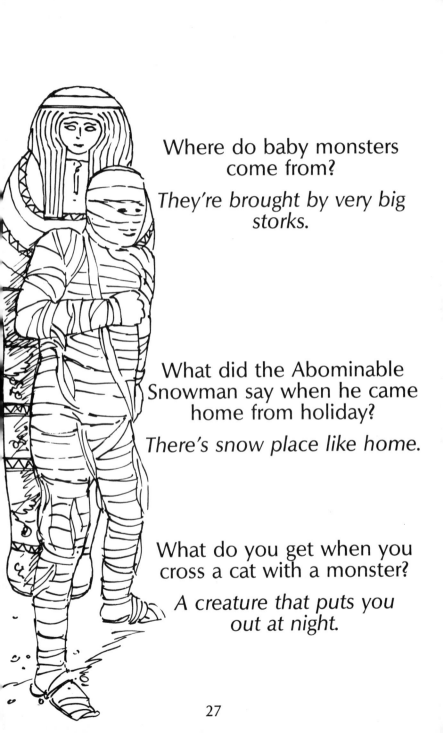

Where do baby monsters come from?

They're brought by very big storks.

What did the Abominable Snowman say when he came home from holiday?

There's snow place like home.

What do you get when you cross a cat with a monster?

A creature that puts you out at night.

27

Which American President ate
people?

Jaws Washington.

What does a monster call his
parents?

Deady and Mummy.

What happens when a
monster sits in front of you
at the cinema?

You miss most of the film.

Why wouldn't the monster
eat Romans?

*Because Italian food
upset him.*

Why did the monster become
a vegetarian?

He got fed up with people.

Why wouldn't the monster eat the people in Bombay?

Because he couldn't stand Indian food.

What do you call a ghost in the fridge?

A real cool ghoul.

How does a monster like its eggs?

Terri-fried.

Where does a 300-kilo
monster sleep?

Anywhere it likes.

How do you know when
a monster's been in
your fridge?

*Great big paw prints in the
butter.*

What did the monster do
when he lost a hand?

*He got a new one from a
second-hand shop.*

What's a monster's favourite game?

Swallow my leader.

What's the difference between a monster and a pillar box?

I don't know?

Well, I'm not going to ask you to post *my* letters.

What does a monster do when it rains?

Gets wet.

Where did the Abominable Snowman meet his wife?

At a snow ball.

What does a short-sighted ghost wear?

Spooktacles.

Why did the ghost go into hospital?

To have his ghoulstones removed.

That girl monster over there just rolled her eyes at me.

Well, roll them back, then.

What's covered with hair, has three eyes, slimy fangs, and hops up and down?

A monster on a pogo stick.

What sort of eyes do monsters have?

Terror-ise.

Why don't monsters eat priests?

Because you can't keep a good man down.

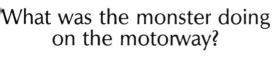

What was the monster doing on the motorway?

Seventy miles an hour.

How do monsters count to thirty?

On their fingers.

What monster swings from tree to tree wearing a dress?

Queen Kong.

Mummy, Mummy, I've brought a friend home for dinner?

Well, pop him in the oven and I'll lay the table.

What happened when the prehistoric monster took his exams?

He passed with extinction.

Why did King Kong join the Army?

He wanted to learn about gorilla warfare.

How did the monster feel after he'd gobbled a herd of sheep?

Very Ba-a-a-d.

Any luck on your monster hunt?

Yes, we didn't find one!

What do you get if you cross a monster with a Boy Scout?

Something horrible that helps old ladies across the road.

What would you find in a haunted pub?

Whines and spirits.

First Monster: I don't feel too well?

Second Monster: *Was it someone you ate.*

What monster gets right up your nose?

A bogeyman.

Mother Monster to Baby Monster: I won't tell you again — don't speak with your mouths full!

What would you give a monster with big feet?

Plenty of room.

Who gives lessons to young monsters?

A ghoulmaster.

What jewels do ghosts wear?

Tomb-stones.

What happens when a
monster sneezes?

You duck.

What does Frankenstein's
monster call a screwdriver?

Daddy.

What's the time when a giant monster sits on your fence?

Time to get a new fence.

What aftershave do monsters use?

Brute.

How do you raise a monster?

With a very big crane.

What monster smells horrible?

King Pong.

Three monsters were
sheltering under an umbrella
but none of them got wet.
Why not?

It wasn't raining.

What's the difference between
a monster and a peanut butter
sandwich?

*Monsters don't stick to the roof
of your mouth.*

Where do monsters eat?

At a beastro.

What do you call a crowd of monsters walking down the street?

A demon-stration.

What's a monster's favourite
meal?

Bangers and baked beings.

First Monster: You look
terrible.

Second Monster: *Thanks for
the compliment.*

What does a grape do when a
monster treads on it?

It just lets out a little whine.

What did the monster say when he saw two monster-hunters in a jeep?

Good — meals on wheels!

What do you call a good-looking, kind, vegetarian monster?

A total failure.

What's the difference between a monster and a flea?

A monster can have fleas but the flea can't have monsters.

Sign outside a monster's
house:

TRESPASSERS WILL BE EATEN.

What did the monster say
when it ate a roll of movie
film?

I preferred the book.

Young Abominable Snowman:
Are you sure I'm an
Abominable Snowman?

Mother Snowman:
Of course you are.
Why do you ask?

Young Abominable Snowman:
Because I'm freezing!

What's a monster's favourite
soup?

One with lots of body in it.

Mother Monster: Why did you put a toad in your sister's bed?

Boy Monster: *'Cos I couldn't find a snake.*

First Girl Monster: I'm still going out with the Invisible Man?

Second Girl Monster: *Don't know what you see in him.*

Who won last year's monster beauty contest?

Can't remember her name, but her measurements were

36.33.37 . . . 35.25.34 . . . 54.44.40 — and that was just her head!

How did the two monsters fall in love?

It was love at first fright.

What do you call a monster wearing earmuffs?

Anything you like, he can't hear you.

What's the best way to catch a monster?

Get someone to throw one to you.

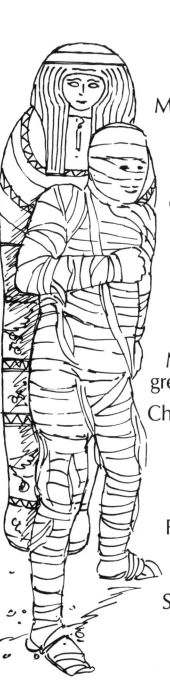

Mummy, Mummy, why do I keep going round and round in circles?

*Be quiet,
or I'll nail your other foot
to the floor.*

Mother Monster: Eat your greens, they're good for you?

Child Monster: *But Mum, you know I don't like frogs.*

First Sailor: Have you ever seen a man-eating sea monster?

Second Sailor: *No, but I've seen a man eating fish.*

Mother Monster: What are you doing?

Child Monster: *I'm chasing a man around a tree.*

Mother Monster: How many times have I told you not to play with your food.

Why does Frankenstein's monster take good care of his hands?

To stop his nails going rusty.

What do ghost-busters write in?

Exorcise books.

What's a monster's favourite meal?

Shepherd's pie — with real shepherds.

What would you say if you
saw a ghost?

AAAAAAARRRGHH!

What did the barman say to
the ghost?

*Sorry, we don't serve spirits
here.*

Where did the lady monster
have her hair done?

At the ugly parlour.

Where does a 500-kilo
monster sleep?

Anywhere it likes.

When do ghosts
play practical jokes?

On April Ghoul's Day.

Why is a locked door like the
neck of Frankenstein's
monster?

They're both bolted.

What is King Kong's favourite
Christmas song?

Jungle Bells, Jungle Bells.

What time is it when a
monster eats the Prime
Minister?

Ate P.M.

On what side does the
Abominable Snowman have
most hair?

On the outside.

What is a monster's favourite dessert?

Eyes cream.

What is a ghoul's favourite fairground ride?

The roller ghoster.

If you met a horrible hairy monster, what time would it be?

Time to run.

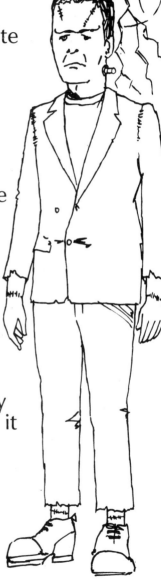

What do you get if you cross a monster with a pair of spiked shoes?

A very angry monster.

Why did the 50-metre hairy monster wear sunglasses?

He didn't want to be recognised.

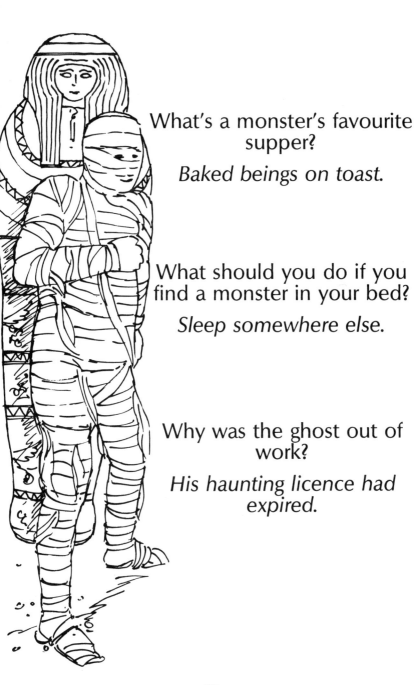

What's a monster's favourite supper?

Baked beings on toast.

What should you do if you find a monster in your bed?

Sleep somewhere else.

Why was the ghost out of work?

His haunting licence had expired.

How do monsters tell fortunes?

They use horror-scopes.

What happened when the monsters ate a comedian?

They had a feast of fun.

What's a monster's skin used for?

To keep the monster inside.

What does a ghost enjoy?
Being shrouded in mystery.

How does a monster
try to go faster?

*He puts his
beast foot forward.*

ow do you talk to a monster?
Use big words.

Why did the monster eat a
lamp post?

He fancied a light lunch.

What do you say to a tall
monster?

Hi!

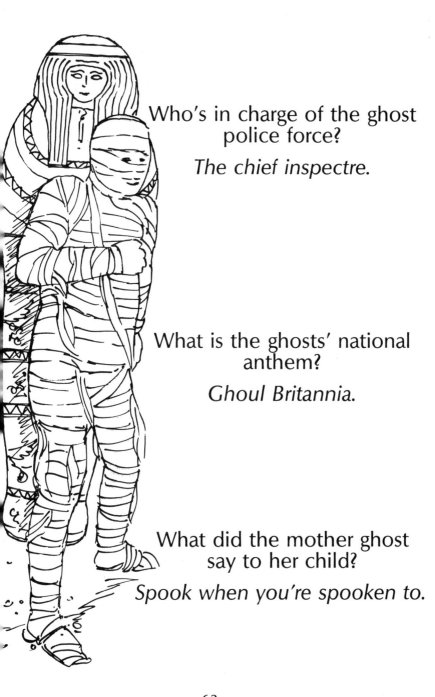

Who's in charge of the ghost police force?

The chief inspectre.

What is the ghosts' national anthem?

Ghoul Britannia.

What did the mother ghost say to her child?

Spook when you're spooken to.

Where do Spanish ghosts go on holiday?

The Ghosta Brava.

What do you call a drunk ghost?

A methylated spirit.

What do you think about the Abominable Snowman?

It leaves me cold.